HISTORY UNCUT

THE REAL

Dolley Madison

Virginia Loh-Hagan

45th Parallel Press

Published in the United States of America by Cherry Lake Publishing
Ann Arbor, Michigan
www.cherrylakepublishing.com

Reading Adviser: Marla Conn MS, Ed., Literacy specialist, Read-Ability, Inc.
Book Designer: Felicia Macheske

Photo Credits: © Raisa Kanareva/Shutterstock.com, cover, 1; Dolley Madison, 1804, by Gilbert Stuart (1755-1828), White House Historical Association, This work is in the public domain in the United States because it was published (or registered with the U.S. Copyright Office) before January 1, 1923. 5, 30; © kzww/Shutterstock.com, 7; © Waravut Wattanapanich/Shutterstock.com, 9; James Madison, 1816, by John Vanderlyn (1775–1852), White House Historical Association, This work is in the public domain in the United States because it was published (or registered with the U.S. Copyright Office) before January 1, 1923. 11; © Dm_Cherry/Shutterstock.com, 12; © Andriy Blokhin/ Shutterstock.com, 15; © Lisa S./Shutterstock.com, 17; © Ingersoll, T. W. White House - Blue Room. Washington D.C, 1898. St. Paul, Minn.: T. W. Ingersoll, Publisher. Photograph. Retrieved from the Library of Congress, https://www.loc.gov/item/2017648911/., 19; © kropic1/Shutterstock.com, 20; © Marzolino/Shutterstock.com, 23; © Eric Isselee/Shutterstock.com, 24; © Veda J Gonzalez/Shutterstock.com, 27; © Orhan Cam/Shutterstock.com, 29

Graphic Elements Throughout: © iulias/Shutterstock.com; © Thinglass/Shutterstock.com; © kzww/Shutterstock.com; © A_Lesik/Shutterstock.com; © MegaShabanov/Shutterstock.com; © Groundback Atelier/Shutterstock.com; © saki80/Shutterstock.com

45th Parallel Press is an imprint of Cherry Lake Publishing.

Library of Congress Cataloging-in-Publication Data

Names: Loh-Hagan, Virginia, author.
Title: Dolley Madison / by Virginia Loh-Hagan.
Description: Ann Arbor, Mich. : Cherry Lake Publishing, 2018. | Series: History uncut | Includes bibliographical references and index.
Identifiers: LCCN 2018004558| ISBN 9781534129528 (hardcover) | ISBN 9781534131224 (pdf) | ISBN 9781534132726 (pbk.) | ISBN 9781534134423 (hosted ebook)
Subjects: LCSH: Madison, Dolley, 1768-1849—Juvenile literature. | Madison, James, 1751-1836—Juvenile literature. | Presidents' spouses—United States—Biography—Juvenile literature.
Classification: LCC E342.1 .L64 2018 | DDC 973.5/1092 [B] –dc23
LC record available at https://lccn.loc.gov/2018004558

Cherry Lake Publishing would like to acknowledge the work of The Partnership for 21st Century Skills. Please visit www.p21.org for more information.

Printed in the United States of America
Corporate Graphics

Table of Contents

Chapter 1
Dolley Madison
The Story You Know 4

Chapter 2
From Quaker Beginnings 6

Chapter 3
The Good Wife 10

Chapter 4
White House Hostess 14

Chapter 5
From Hostess to Heroine 18

Chapter 6
Following the Leader 22

Chapter 7
Partying to the End 26

Timeline 30

Consider This! 31
Learn More 31
Glossary 32
Index 32
About the Author 32

CHAPTER 1

Dolley Madison The Story You Know

Dolley Madison was the wife of a U.S. president. She was the first woman to be called **First Lady**. This is the title of a male president's wife. Madison defined what it meant to be First Lady. She created traditions. She decorated the White House. She hosted events. She worked with local **charities**. Charities are groups that help the poor.

Madison supported her husband. She supported her country. She helped build the nation's style and independence. She was very social. She was very charming. She put people at ease. She won people over.

She paved the way for other first ladies. She was a role model. But there's more to her story...

First Lady is a hard job, but they don't get paid.

CHAPTER 2

From Quaker Beginnings

Madison was born on May 20, 1768. She was the third of 8 children. She was the first girl. Her family was **Quaker**. Quakers are a Christian group. They have many rules. They don't fight. They don't like slavery. They don't dance or play cards. They don't wear fancy clothes or jewelry. They only marry other Quakers. They kick out people who break their rules.

Quakers believe in education. So, Madison learned to read and write. She was more educated than most Americans at this time.

Her father died. So, her mother made money. She opened a boarding home. She served officials. Madison learned how to be around powerful men.

Madison was born in a log cabin.

Setting the World Stage

1768

- Philip Astley was from London. He was a horse rider and inventor. He invented the circus ring. He did this in 1768. He rode in a circle, not a straight line. He did riding tricks. He did stunts in a ring. He hired acrobats, tightrope walkers, jugglers, and clowns. Future circus owners copied his ideas.

- Captain James Cook was an explorer. His first voyage was in 1768. His ship was called the HMS *Endeavor*. He sailed from England. He crossed the Atlantic Ocean. He sailed to the southern Pacific Ocean. He sailed to Australia. This voyage took 3 years.

- Hungli was a Chinese ruler. He made the country rich. He extended China's borders. But he also feared witches. He killed monks and medicine men. He thought they were "soul stealers." This was called the "Great Sorcery Scare of 1768."

"I have always been an advocate for fighting when assailed."
– Dolley Madison

Before he died, Madison's father picked a husband for her. He picked John Todd. Todd was a Quaker. He was a lawyer. He lived in Philadelphia. Madison loved him. She was happy. They had 2 sons.

In 1793, Todd and her second son died. They got **yellow fever**. This is a sickness. It's spread by mosquitoes. It causes fevers. It causes stomach pains. It causes muscle pains. It causes liver damage. This makes the skin yellow. It can be deadly.

Madison became a **widow**. Widows are women whose husbands died. Madison was 25 years old. She had a young son. She needed to support herself.

Over 4,000 people died of yellow fever in Philadelphia.

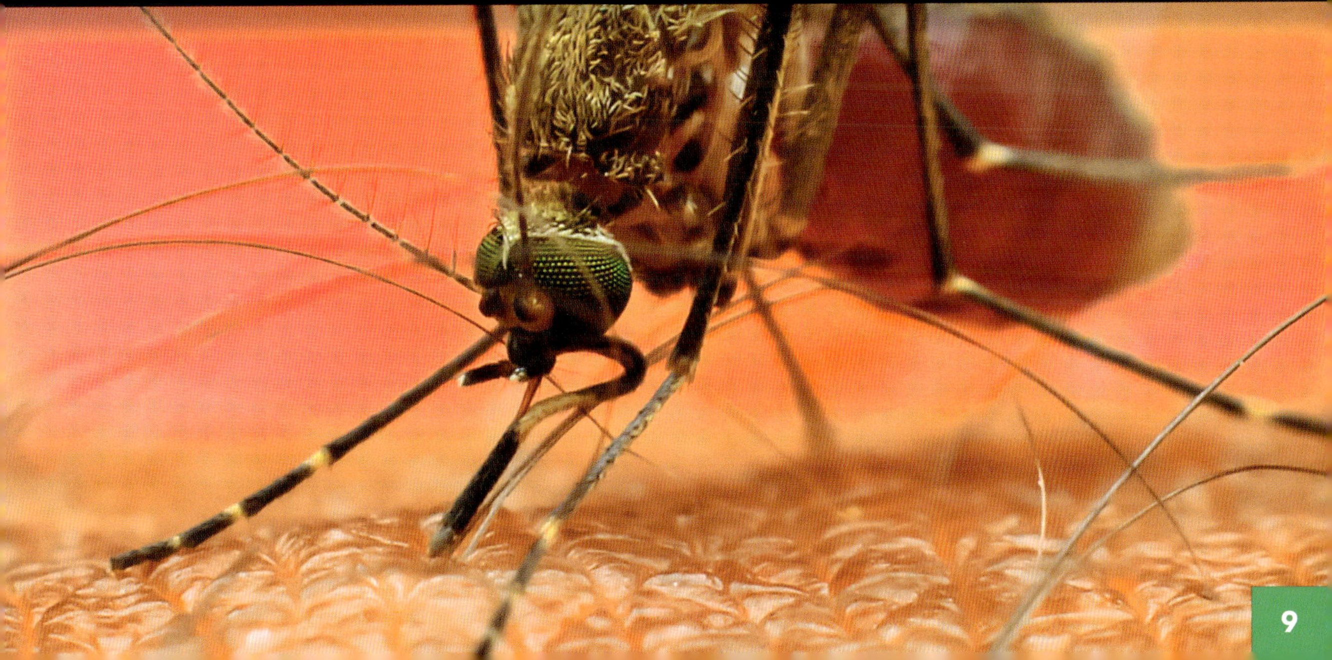

CHAPTER 3

The Good Wife

James Madison was short. He was thin. He was going bald. He was 17 years older than Dolley Madison. He wore black. He spoke in low tones. He wasn't social. He was a Founding Father. He helped create the United States. He was famous. He was rich. He was smart. He was kind. And he loved Dolley Madison.

Madison wasn't in love with him at first. She wouldn't marry him right away. But she finally did. She married him in 1794. He wasn't a Quaker. So, the Quakers disowned Madison.

They were married for 41 years. They were a good match. They rarely fought. They teased each other. They wrote love letters.

James Madison was 2 inches (5 centimeters)
shorter than Dolley Madison.

Madison was more than a good wife. She was also a good partner. She helped James's career. He was quiet. So, Madison did a lot of talking.

She visited new leaders. She hosted "dove parties" for their wives. She took women to sessions in Congress. She took women to sessions at the Supreme Court. She shared information with James. She promoted James to others. She spread good news about him. She helped James. She took notes for him. She took over his duties when he was sick.

Madison and James were partners. But Madison was careful to not act like his equal. Women didn't have many rights. They were not treated fairly.

Women were considered the property of men.

All in the Family

Dolley Madison's only living child was John Payne Todd. Todd was born in 1792. James Madison adopted him when he was 2 years old. Todd went to a Catholic boarding school. He was there for 8 years. But he wasn't a good student. He was not successful like his parents. He drank a lot. He got in a lot of fights. He had shooting accidents. He was jailed several times. He gambled. He owed a lot of money. His parents tried to help him. They paid the money he owed. They got him out of jail. James Madison gave him jobs. But Todd played instead of worked. He made his parents poor. Dolley Madison sold Montpelier to pay Todd's bills. Montpelier was their home. Todd died of typhoid fever. He died 3 years after his mother. He died in 1852. He freed his slaves when he died. This was his most noble act.

"When I shall again write to you, or where I shall be tomorrow, I cannot tell." – Dolley Madison

CHAPTER 4

White House Hostess

Thomas Jefferson became the third U.S. president. He appointed James Madison to be secretary of state. Jefferson's wife had died. He needed help. He asked Dolley Madison to host his parties. She agreed. This happened in 1801.

She met important people. She learned about politics. She supported the Lewis and Clark **Expedition**. Expeditions are missions. This expedition doubled the country's size. Madison helped raise money for it.

She helped James. He was shy. She helped make secretary of state an important position. She helped make James the fourth U.S. president. She celebrated her husband winning the election. She hosted the first presidential **ball**. Balls are fancy parties.

The Madison family lived at Montpelier.
This was the name of the plantation in Virginia.

THAT Happened?!?

Dolley Madison loved wearing turbans. But she wasn't the only one. Avtar Singh Mauni is from India. He has the largest turban. His turban is made of over 2,000 feet (610 meters) of cloth. It's shaped like a tower. It uses over 100 hairpins. It has over 50 metal religious symbols. It weighs 100 pounds (45 kilograms). It takes 6 hours to put on. Mauni adds to it. He's been doing so for 16 years. He feels incomplete without it. He said, "Until the time I have no more have strength in my limbs, I will carry this turban on my head." Robert Lewis also loves turbans. He's from Canada. He has the largest collection of caps and turbans. He has 2,345 caps and turbans. His collection has different styles. The hats are from different time periods. The hats are made of different materials.

"There is a secret in life, better than anything a fortune teller can reveal. We all have a great hand in the forming of our own destiny." – Dolley Madison

Madison hosted many dinner parties. She hosted more than any other First Lady. She sat at the head of the table. Her table was called "America's Table." She served fancy foods. She served local foods.

She started "Mrs. Madison's Wednesday Nights." These were parties. Anyone could come. People could talk to her and James. These parties were called **squeezes**. Hundreds of people came. People squeezed in. Her parties were fun. She partied with purpose. People shared news. They made connections.

Madison never forgot a name or face. She invited women to her parties. She wanted people to get along. She wanted people to come together.

Madison asked other wives for recipes.

CHAPTER 5

From Hostess to Heroine

Madison helped make Washington, D.C., into the nation's capital. D.C. was a new city. It was being built. It was muddy. It was mostly swamp. Madison's parties made it the place to be.

Madison wanted the United States to be powerful. She proved Americans were just as grand as Europeans. She turned the White House into a national symbol. She fixed up the White House. She put up new wallpaper. She bought new furniture. She bought a piano. She bought things made in America.

Congress gave her money to decorate the White House.

The War of 1812 happened. The British wanted to get America back. British soldiers bombed the city.

Madison still hosted parties. She calmed people. She invited U.S. troops in for snacks. She let everyone know her husband would win the war.

The White House came under attack. People ran. Madison said, "I am not afraid of anything." She saved important papers. She saved a famous picture of George Washington. She told servants to break the frame. She grabbed the picture. She sent it to a safe place. She fled the White House. The British burned it down.

Madison created a spy deck on the White House roof. She watched for British troops.

Bad Blood

Siena College Research Institute is in New York. It was founded in 1980. It conducts opinion polls. It studies many issues. It rates U.S. first ladies. Dolley Madison is always one of the top first ladies. But she's not the top pick. Eleanor Roosevelt usually wins the first spot. Roosevelt was married to Franklin D. Roosevelt. She was First Lady from 1933 to 1945. She was called the "First Lady of the World." She changed the role of the First Lady. She was involved in politics. She helped her husband lead the country. She fought for human rights. She held press conferences. She wrote newspaper articles. She spoke at national meetings. She served in the United Nations. She worked for the American Red Cross. She was one of the most publicly outspoken first ladies.

"I would rather fight with my hands than my tongue."

—Dolley Madison

CHAPTER 6

Following the Leader

Madison was a leader. She believed in the United States. She fought hard to build it. People wanted to move the capital. They wanted to move away from D.C. Madison pushed to stay in D.C. People listened to her. She showed how strong America was.

She set **trends**. Trends are fads and styles. People copied her. They were inspired by her. For example, she wore **turbans**. Turbans are types of hats. They're made by wrapping cloth around the head. Madison stuck feathers in them. She could be easily seen. Other women started wearing turbans.

She was friends with important women in France.
So, she wore all the new French fashions.

She introduced ice cream. She served it at the White House. Keeping things cold was expensive. So, this was a big deal. She made ice cream popular. (Her favorite was oyster ice cream. But she served strawberry ice cream more.)

She also made parrots popular pets. Madison's parrot was named Polly. Polly sat on Madison's shoulder. She greeted people. She spoke. Sometimes, she said bad words. She dived at people. She attacked. Once, she even bit James's finger.

Madison's good deeds were copied. She raised money to help the poor. She raised money for education. Other women did the same.

Polly was a conversation-starter. People wanted to talk about the parrot.

CHAPTER 7

Partying to the End

James retired. The Madisons moved to Virginia. James became sick. Dolley took care of him. James died in 1836.

Her son had a lot of **debt**. Debt is money owed. Madison paid his debts. This made her poor. She had to sell the family home. She sold her husband's papers.

She spent her last years in D.C. She lived close to the White House. She was welcomed. Many people threw parties for her. New first ladies visited her. They wanted to learn from her. They asked her for advice.

Her last public appearance was at a White House party. She was President James K. Polk's special guest.

Madison's presence at a party was much sought after.

Explained by SCIENCE

Dolley Madison was an extrovert. Extroverts are social. Carl Jung was a psychologist. He studied human behavior. He came up with the words introvert and extrovert. Introverts are not social. Hans Eysenck was also a psychologist. He said introverts need less stimulation to be happy. He said extroverts need more excitement. Extroverts need to be around people. They need new experiences. They get energy from social activity. Dopamine is a chemical. It's released in the brain. It gives a burst of energy. It makes people talk more. It makes people take more risks. Both introverts and extroverts have the same amount of dopamine. But dopamine is more active in extroverts' brains.

"It is one of my sources of happiness never to desire a knowledge of other people's business." – Dolley Madison

She had a special seat in Congress. She's the only First Lady to have this honor.

She responded to a **telegraph** message. She was the first private citizen to do so. Telegraphs send messages. They led to the invention of radios and phones.

She got free stamps. This meant she could send mail. Sending mail was expensive at this time.

She died in 1849. She was 81 years old. She had the largest funeral at that time. Everyone wanted to go. The city shut down to honor her. President Zachary Taylor called her the "First Lady." This was the first time this title was used. Madison was a special woman. Everyone loved her because she loved everyone.

Madison was a symbol of early American government.

Timeline

1768 Madison was born. She was born in Guilford County, North Carolina. Her name was Dolley Payne.

1769 Madison's family moved to Hanover County, Virginia.

1783 Madison's father freed his slaves. The family moved to Philadelphia. They started a new business. The business failed. Her father became very sad.

1790 Madison married John Todd. They got married at the Pine Street Meeting House.

1792 Madison gave birth to her son. His name was John Payne Todd.

1793 Madison gave birth to her second son. His name was William Temple Todd. Madison's husband and William died from yellow fever. Madison got sick. But she lived.

1794 Madison met James Madison. Aaron Burr introduced them.

1794 Madison married James Madison. She was kicked out of the Quaker community.

1797 Madison moved to Montpelier. This was Madison's plantation. It's in Virginia.

1801 Madison moved to Washington, D.C.

1809 Madison was the first to host a Presidential Inaugural Ball in Washington, D.C.

1809 Madison bought the first piano for the White House. She paid $450.

1812 Madison hosted the first wedding at the White House. Her sister, Lucy, married Thomas Todd. Todd was a Supreme Court justice.

1844 Madison sold Montpelier. She moved back to Washington, D.C.

1849 Madison died. She was buried in the Congressional Cemetery. She wanted to be buried with James at Montpelier. But she no longer owned Montpelier.

1858 Madison was buried again. Her body was moved to Montpelier.

Consider This!

Take a Position! Some people didn't like Dolley Madison. They thought she was too vocal. They thought she was silly. They thought she was too involved. What do you think? Argue your point with reasons and evidence.

Say What? Dolley Madison was the first First Lady. Learn about another First Lady. Compare them. Explain how they're the same. Explain how they're different.

Think About It! A male president's wife is called the First Lady. What should a female president's husband be called? Why do you think so?

Learn More

Kent, Zachary. *Dolley Madison: "The Enemy Cannot Frighten a Free People."* Berkeley Heights, NJ: Enslow Publishers, 2010.

Krull, Kathleen. *Women Who Broke the Rules: Dolley Madison*. New York: Bloomsbury, 2015.

Oachs, Emily Rose. *Dolley Madison: Hostess and Patriot*. Mankato, MN: Child's World, 2018.

Glossary

ball (BAWL) a fancy party

charities (CHAR-ih-teez) groups that help the poor by raising money or providing services

debt (DET) money owed

expedition (ek-spuh-DISH-uhn) mission or journey with a purpose

First Lady (FURST LAY-dee) title given to the wife of a male U.S. president or state governor

Quaker (KWAY-kur) a Christian group that prefers simple religious services and opposes war

squeezes (SKWEEZ-iz) name of Dolley Madison's parties because people had to squeeze in since there were so many attendees

telegraph (TEL-ih-graf) a way of sending long-distance messages; led to inventions such as the phone and radio

trends (TRENDZ) fads or styles

turbans (TUR-buhnz) headwear made by wrapping cloth around and around

widow (WID-oh) woman whose husband has died

yellow fever (YEL-oh FEE-vur) a disease that is spread by infected mosquitoes

Index

Burr, Aaron, 30

extrovert, 28

First Lady, 4, 5, 17, 21, 29, 31

ice cream, 25

Madison, James, 10–14, 17, 25, 26, 30

Quakers, 6, 9, 10, 30

Roosevelt, Eleanor, 21

Todd, John, 9, 30

Todd, John Payne, 13, 30

turbans, 16, 22

War of 1812, 20

White House, 4, 14, 18—20, 25, 26, 30

About the Author

Dr. Virginia Loh-Hagan is an author, university professor, former classroom teacher, and curriculum designer. Like Dolley, she loves hosting parties. She lives in San Diego with her very tall husband and very naughty dogs. To learn more about her, visit www.virginialoh.com.